Notes
of
Gratitude

Copyright

All rights reserved. Without limiting the rights under copyright reserved above, no part of this publication may be reproduced, stored in or introduced into a retrieval system, or transmitted, in any other form or by any means (electronic, mechanical, photocopying, recording or otherwise), without the permission of both the copyright owner and the publisher of this book. Except in the case of brief quotations embodied in critical reviews and specific other non-commercial uses permitted by copyright law.

Created by: NikkNakk Designs
With immense gratitude to my family and friends who love and support me with my creative adventures.

First published in 2019
© 2019 Westminster Designs Pty Ltd
ISBN 978-1-925422-23-8

Foreword

Notes of Gratitude is a carefully designed journal for self-reflection, inside, you will find a scattering of little memory joggers to help you remember things for which you can be grateful. Plus a liberal sprinkling of blank pages for you to complete with free will.

Feeling grateful is the art of appreciation by focusing on the good things in your life. This creates more positive feelings and more positive thoughts about the future.

Many studies have shown the many benefits, an attitude of gratitude may generate, these include;

1. **More loving and quality relationships.**

2. **An improvement in physical health, including sleeping, longer and better.**

3. **Improved self-esteem and confidence.**

4. **People who practice gratitude feel more relaxed, happy and calm.**

5. **Reduced anxiety and depression.**

6. **Grateful people exercise more and have more vitality.**

7. **Gratitude increases mental strength and resilience.**

Being thankful is something I try to do every day either first thing in the morning to set my intention to have a happy, positive day or at night to give thanks for the great moments and people in my life.

I also express random acts of gratitude throughout the day when something wonderful happens unexpectedly.

One thing I am grateful for is inspirational quotes. Two of my favourites are listed below;

"In the midst of winter, I found there was, within me, an invincible summer." Albert Camus

This inspirational quote by Albert Camus is a reminder I can handle anything that comes my way!

I created this book to help others find their 'Attitude of Gratitude.' You don't have to do it every day, but like most things the more you do, the better you get at it and then it becomes second nature. Daily gratitude practice will soon become a way of life that you will enjoy and from which you will receive huge benefits.

Some people will work their way through the book from beginning to end - completing each page, others will randomly open the book and complete the page in front of them. There is NO right or wrong, simply do what feels good for you. This journal has enough pages to be used every day for three months, there is plenty of space to write thoughts and reflections or include photos or pictures.

We don't have to personally experience a happy moment we simply have to notice them. When you see someone else experience joy and happiness, it can have the same positive impact as if we experienced it ourselves.

"At times, our own light goes out and is rekindled by a spark from another person. Each of us has cause to think with deep gratitude of those who have lighted the flame within us." A Schweitzer

This quote by A Schweitzer reminds me to thank (and be grateful for) the people who assist me on my journey.

I hope you find inspiration in these quotes and this book helps you to find more joyful moments every day.

Date   /   /

Today was positively packed with many beautiful moments, including ...

Date   /   /

Today I am grateful for...

Date   /   /

Today I am grateful for...

Date   /   /

I am thankful I can set goals in my life and work towards them every day to help me achieve more in life, including ....

Date   /   /

Today I am grateful for...

Date   /   /

Today I am grateful for...

Date   /   /

Today was fun and happy with many beautiful moments, including ...

Date   /   /

Today I am grateful for...

Date   /   /

Today I am grateful for...

Date   /   /

Today I celebrate my day and am thankful for the great things in my life, including ...

Date   /   /

Today I am grateful for...

Date   /   /

Today I am grateful for...

Date   /   /

I am happy I am strong enough to work through any challenges in life and overcome them such as ....

Date   /   /

Today I am grateful for...

Date   /   /

Today I am grateful for...

Date   /   /

Today I am grateful for my family and the special moments we share and enjoy.

Date   /   /

Today I am grateful for...

Date   /   /

Today I am grateful for...

Date   /   /

The best thing about today was ...

Date   /   /

Today I am grateful for...

Date   /   /

Today I am grateful for...

Date   /   /

Today I celebrate the beauty of nature, especially ...

Date   /   /

Today I am grateful for...

Date   /   /

Today I am grateful for...

Date   /   /

Today I am grateful for my past and the lessons I have learnt which make me a better person in so many ways.

Date   /   /

Today I am grateful for...

Date   /   /

Today I am grateful for...

Date   /   /

I am lucky to have a job that provides for my self and family, what I enjoy about my career the most is ...

Date   /   /

Today I am grateful for...

Date   /   /

Today I am grateful for...

Date   /   /

I am grateful I have lovely friends to share lots of happy moments.

Date   /   /

Today I am grateful for...

Date   /   /

Today I am grateful for...

Date   /   /

Soon I will thank ...

Date   /   /

Today I am grateful for...

Date   /   /

Today I am grateful for...

Date   /   /

Today I am grateful I have all five senses, so I can hear, touch, smell, taste and see.

Date   /   /

Today I am grateful for...

Date   /   /

Today I am grateful for...

Date   /   /

Today I choose to be happy,
even if life is not going according to plan.

Date   /   /

Today I am grateful for...

Date   /   /

Today I am grateful for...

Date   /   /

I am thankful for my children and the delight and colour they bring to my life.

Date   /   /

Today I am grateful for...

Date   /   /

Today I am grateful for...

Date   /   /

Today I am thankful for my comfortable bed and having a safe place to sleep.

Date   /   /

Today I am grateful for...

Date   /   /

Today I am grateful for...

Date   /   /

I appreciate my boss and co-workers and how they make my work day more enjoyable.

Date   /   /

Today I am grateful for...

Date   /   /

Today I am grateful for...

Date   /   /

Today I am grateful for the smiles of strangers.

Date   /   /

Today I am grateful for...

Date   /   /

Today I am grateful for...

Date   /   /

Today I celebrate the innovations of technology and how they have made people's lives easier.

Date   /   /

Today I am grateful for...

Date   /   /

Today I am grateful for...

Date   /   /

Today I am grateful for the kindness of others, including ...

Date   /   /

Today I am grateful for...

Date   /   /

Today I am grateful for...

Date   /   /

Today I am grateful for the Doctors and Nurses who work so hard to help people feel better.

Date   /   /

Today I am grateful for...

Date   /   /

Today I am grateful for...

Date   /   /

I enjoy the warm sunny days of summer when I can ...

Date   /   /

Today I am grateful for...

Date   /   /

Today I am grateful for...

Date   /   /

Today I am grateful that I got to make a difference in someone else's life by doing ....

Date   /   /

Today I am grateful for...

Date   /   /

Today I am grateful for...

Date   /   /

I am thankful that I can watch my family grow up ...

Date   /   /

Today I am grateful for...

Date   /   /

Today I am grateful for...

Date   /   /

Today I am grateful for the rain which refreshes my garden.

Date   /   /

Today I am grateful for...

Date   /   /

Today I am grateful for...

Date   /   /

Today I am grateful for the failures in my life and the lessons I have learnt.

Date   /   /

Today I am grateful for...

Date   /   /

Today I am grateful for...

Date   /   /

At this moment I celebrate the love in my life from all its different sources.

Date   /   /

Today I am grateful for...

Date   /   /

Today I am grateful for...

Date   /   /

Today I am celebrating my successes in life, including ...

Date   /   /

Today I am grateful for...

Date   /   /

Today I am grateful for...

Date   /   /

I am thankful I have a wonderful partner with whom I share many joyful moments.

Date   /   /

Today I am grateful for...

Date   /   /

Today I am grateful for...

Date   /   /

Today I am grateful for finding a parking spot when I am in a hurry.

Date   /   /

Today I am grateful for...

Date   /   /

Today I am grateful for...

Date   /   /

I am grateful I learnt the lesson of ...

Date   /   /

Today I am grateful for...

Date   /   /

Today I am grateful for...

Date   /   /

Today I am grateful for the courage I have in the face of adversity.

Date   /   /

Today I am grateful for...

Date   /   /

Today I am grateful for...

Date   /   /

Today I am grateful for my pets and the joy they bring into my life.

Date   /   /

Today I am grateful for...

Date   /   /

Today I am grateful for...

Date   /   /

Today I am grateful for the abundance of nourishing food that supports my body.

Date   /   /

Today I am grateful for...

Date   /   /

Today I am grateful for...

Date   /   /

Today I am grateful for how good I feel when I exercise.

Date   /   /

Today I am grateful for...

Date   /   /

Today I am grateful for...

Date   /   /

Today I am grateful for my favourite place in nature and how I feel when I am there.

Date   /   /

Today I am grateful for...

Date   /   /

Today I am grateful for...

Other Books by NikkNakk Designs include:

Glowing with Gratitude

Fairies and Flowers Adult Colouring Book

Progressive Patterns for Men

Progressive Patterns for Busy Mothers

www.ingramcontent.com/pod-product-compliance
Lightning Source LLC
Chambersburg PA
CBHW021116080526
44587CB00010B/535